Across

1. Large in size or amount
2. Develop
3. Easily deceived
4. Containing, tasting of, or similar to nuts
5. Extremely large
6. Level and smooth
7. Unhappy or sorry

Down

8. Fashionable and interesting
9. Disapproving, wishing to fight or argue
10. Gradually and secretly causing harm
11. Revealing
12. Not in danger or likely to be harmed

Across

1. Unkind, cruel
2. Dark and dirty or difficult to see through
3. Complicated and difficult to solve
4. Unkind, cruel, without sympathy
5. Full of people
6. Extremely large
7. Often forgetting things
8. Able to send back light a surface
9. Ordinary or usual

Down

10. Eager to fight or argue
11. Attractive or pleasant
12. Hing, or activity could harm you
13. Not the same
14. Without a home
15. Not in danger or likely to be harmed
16. Develop

Across

1. Accepted, accept something
2. Easily deceived
3. Glue
4. Containing, tasting of, or similar to nuts
5. Broken part
6. Not guilty of aparticular crime
7. Relating to love or a close loving relationship
8. Not bitter or salty
9. Extremely surprising, very good, extremely surprised
10. Difficult to understand
11. No water or other liquid in

Down

12. Fashionable and interesting
13. Hard or firm
14. Very respected
15. Develop
16. Impossible to defeat
17. Disapproving, wishing to fight or argue
18. Unwilling to give information
19. Showing much knowledge
20. Ordinary or usual
21. Dissolves materials

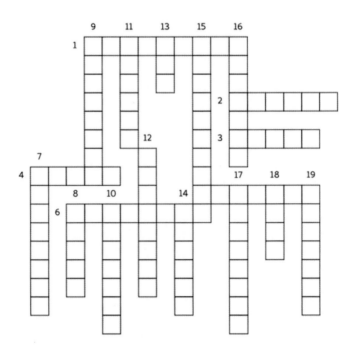

Across

1. Gradually and secretly causing harm
2. Stupid,unreasonable, silly in a humorous way, things that happen that are unreasonable
3. Respecting God
4. Containing, tasting of, or similar to nuts
5. Not armed
6. Without a home

Down

7. Not clear and having no form
8. Unkind, cruel
9. Not guilty of aparticular crime
10. Gigantic prehistoric animal
11. Immediately after the first and before any others
12. Easily deceived
13. No water or other liquid in
14. Rightened or worried
15. Unacceptable, offensive, violent, or unusual
16. Unusual and unexpected
17. Glue
18. Nothing more than
19. Refusing to obey

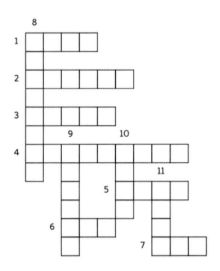

Across

1. Boring
2. Rightened or worried
3. Shaped like a ball or circle
4. Limited to only one person
5. Level and smooth
6. Large in size or amount
7. No water or other liquid in

Down

8. Careful not to attract too much attention
9. Rounded in a pleasant and attractive way
10. Not in danger or likely to be harmed
11. Dissolves materials

Across

1. Someone who is trying to become successful
2. On or onto a ship, aircraft, bus, or train
3. Rounded in a pleasant and attractive way
4. Revealing
5. Able to produce the intended result
6. Careful not to attract too much attention

Down

7. Happy and positive
8. Not armed
9. Attractive, appealing, lovely, charming, and easily loved
10. Coming before all others
11. Not decorated in any way; with nothing added
12. A foolish idea
13. Strong and unlikely to break or fail
14. Extremely surprising, very good, extremely surprised
15. Not far away in distance
16. Extremely large
17. Intentionally choosing some things and not others
18. Happening or done quickly and without warning

Across

1. a phone who uses that
2. On or onto a ship, aircraft, bus, or train
3. Dissolves materials
4. Not far away in distance
5. Complain in an angry way
6. No water or other liquid in
7. Shaped like a ball or circle
8. Rounded in a pleasant and attractive way
9. Not armed
10. Unhappy or sorry
11. Not bitter or salty
12. Level and smooth
13. Very respected
14. Containing, tasting of, or similar to nuts

Down

15. Not in danger or likely to be harmed
16. Behave like adults
17. Happy and positive
18. Damaged
19. Showing much knowledge
20. Strong and unlikely to break or fail
21. Harmed or spoiled
22. Hing, or activity could harm you
23. Detestable, repugnant, repulsive, morally very bad
24. Beautiful, powerful, or causing great admiration and respect
25. Loved very much

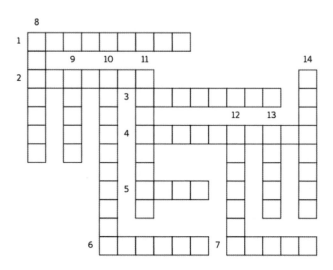

Across

1. Gradually and secretly causing harm
2. Gigantic prehistoric animal
3. Glue
4. Very pleasant
5. Man
6. Happening or done quickly and without warning
7. Hard or firm

Down

8. Extremely large
9. Dark and dirty or difficult to see through
10. Unacceptable, offensive, violent, or unusual
11. Physically attractive
12. Extremely ugly or bad
13. Coming before all others
14. Very respected

Across

1. Harmed or spoiled
2. Ability to do an activity or job well
3. Fashionable and interesting
4. Complicated and difficult to solve
5. Not armed

Down

6. Unhappy or sorry
7. Containing, tasting of, or similar to nuts
8. Very pleasant
9. Extremely surprising, very good, extremely surprised
10. Behave like adults
11. Happening or done quickly and without warning
12. Loved very much

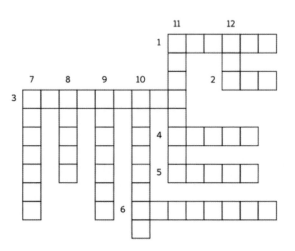

Across

1. Rounded in a pleasant and attractive way
2. No water or other liquid in
3. Limited to only one person
4. Coming before all others
5. At the same height
6. Not clear and having no form

Down

7. Able to stretch
8. Causing pain intentionally
9. Not armed
10. Not guilty of aparticular crime
11. Happy and positive
12. Unpleasant and causing difficulties or harm, evil, low quality, not acceptable

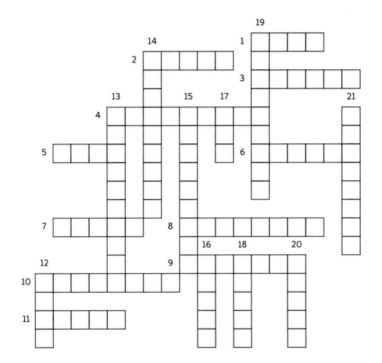

Across

1. Dissolves materials
2. Drinking too much alcohol
3. Strong and unlikely to break or fail
4. Broken part
5. Having a value of zero
6. Damaged
7. Containing, tasting of, or similar to nuts
8. Inside the body
9. Able to stretch
10. Ability to do an activity or job well
11. Coming before all others

Down

12. Not in danger or likely to be harmed
13. Very pleasant
14. Not the same
15. Eager to fight or argue
16. At the same height
17. Extremely cold
18. Not bitter or salty
19. Accepted, accept something
20. Not dirty
21. Not guilty of aparticular crime

Across

1. No water or other liquid in
2. Not bitter or salty
3. Able to send back light a surface
4. Complete and correct in every way, of the best possible type or without fault
5. Develop
6. At the same height
7. Coming before all others
8. Not clear and having no form
9. Ability to do an activity or job well
10. Unhappy or sorry

Down

11. Having a lot of power to control people and events
12. Detestable, repugnant, repulsive, morally very bad
13. Careful not to attract too much attention
14. Revealing
15. Most excellent, highest quality,
16. Happy and positive
17. Not in danger or likely to be harmed

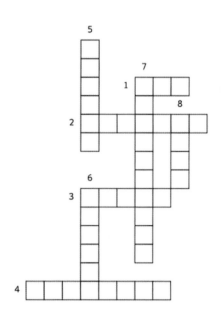

Across

1. No water or other liquid in
2. Revealing
3. Containing, tasting of, or similar to nuts
4. Easily deceived

Down

5. Complicated and difficult to solve
6. Ordinary or usual
7. Very pleasant
8. Not far away in distance

Across
1. Officer
2. The color of chocolate
3. Shaped like a ball or circle
4. Not bitter or salty
5. Dissolves materials
6. Hard or firm
7. Extremely surprising, very good, extremely surprised
8. Loved very much
9. Expressing thanks
10. Unhappy or sorry

Down
11. Unusual and unexpected
12. Damaged, break
13. Fashionable and interesting
14. Ordinary or usual
15. Gradually and secretly causing harm

Across

1. Happy or grateful because of something
2. Extremely ugly or bad
3. Able to stretch
4. Relating to love or a close loving relationship
5. Revealing
6. Respecting God
7. Careful not to attract too much attention
8. Coming before all others

Down

9. Feel slightly drunk
10. Loved very much
11. Not in danger or likely to be harmed
12. Attractive or pleasant
13. Not wanting others to know
14. Said or thought by some people to be the stated bad or illegal thing, although you have no proof
15. At the same height

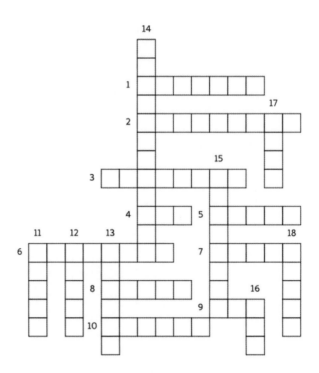

Across
1. Able to stretch
2. Attractive or pleasant
3. Not guilty of aparticular crime
4. Large in size or amount
5. The color of chocolate
6. Careful not to attract too much attention
7. Telling not the true
8. Unhappy because you have nothing to do
9. Unhappy or sorry
10. Rightened or worried

Down
11. Drinking too much alcohol
12. Not bitter or salty
13. Strong and unlikely to break or fail
14. Not certain, or wrong in some way
15. Not clear and having no form
16. No water or other liquid in
17. Nothing more than
18. Respecting God

Across

1. Drinking too much alcohol
2. Not bitter or salty
3. Complicated and difficult to solve
4. Telling not the true
5. Develop
6. No water or other liquid in
7. Not dirty

Down

8. Not far away in distance
9. Broken part
10. Relating to love or a close loving relationship
11. Ordinary or usual
12. With clouds
13. Not guilty of aparticular crime

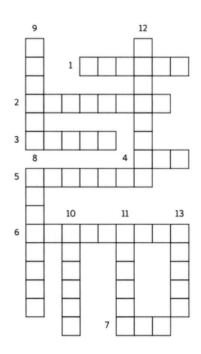

Across

1. Fashionable and interesting
2. Careful not to attract too much attention
3. Containing, tasting of, or similar to nuts
4. Unhappy or sorry
5. Unkind, cruel, without sympathy
6. Limited to only one person
7. No water or other liquid in

Down

8. Happy and positive
9. Happening or done quickly and without warning
10. Fact that everyone knows
11. Rightened or worried
12. Without a home
13. Develop

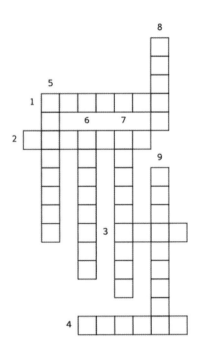

Across

1. Extremely large
2. Not armed
3. Not in danger or likely to be harmed
4. Complicated and difficult to solve

Down

5. Not guilty of aparticular crime
6. Relating to love or a close loving relationship
7. Limited to only one person
8. Not bitter or salty
9. Not the same

Across

1. A foolish idea
2. Not far away in distance
3. Inside the body
4. Not armed
5. Develop
6. Fashionable and interesting
7. Level and smooth
8. At the same height

Down

9. Not guilty of aparticular crime
10. Worried, nervous
11. Someone who is trying to become successful
12. a phone who uses that
13. Very pleasant
14. Complicated and difficult to solve

Across

1. Not bitter or salty
2. Hard or firm
3. Careful not to attract too much attention
4. Detestable, repugnant, repulsive, morally very bad
5. Not far away in distance
6. Unkind, cruel, without sympathy

Down

7. Happening or done quickly and without warning
8. Immediately after the first and before any others
9. Worried, nervous
10. Not in danger or likely to be harmed
11. Very well
12. Make something more likely to happen
13. Having a pleasant smell

Across
1. Grand very large
2. Unhappy because you have nothing to do
3. Strong and unlikely to break or fail
4. Containing, tasting of, or similar to nuts
5. At the same height
6. Not guilty of aparticular crime

Down
7. The color of chocolate
8. Habit of talking a lot
9. Drinking too much alcohol
10. Happening or done quickly and without warning
11. Revealing
12. Fashionable and interesting
13. Not bitter or salty

Across

1. Immediately after the first and before any others
2. Causing pain intentionally
3. Not smooth
4. Not clear and having no form

Down

5. Unpleasant and causing difficulties or harm, evil, low quality, not acceptable
6. Fact that everyone knows
7. Attractive in appearance
8. Not bitter or salty
9. Not armed
10. Attractive or pleasant
11. Happening or done quickly and without warning
12. Not far away in distance

Across

1. On or onto a ship, aircraft, bus, or train
2. Feel slightly drunk
3. Happy and positive
4. Gradually and secretly causing harm
5. Attractive or pleasant
6. Abnormal, deviant, different

Down

7. Not dirty
8. Make something more likely to happen
9. Detestable, repugnant, repulsive, morally very bad
10. Attractive in appearance
11. Not excited
12. Containing, tasting of, or similar to nuts
13. Immediately after the first and before any others
14. a phone who uses that

Across

1. Not in danger or likely to be harmed
2. Extremely large
3. Attractive, appealing, lovely, charming, and easily loved
4. Not armed
5. On or onto a ship, aircraft, bus, or train
6. Unhappy or sorry
7. At the same height
8. Easily deceived
9. Harmed or spoiled

Down

10. Worried, nervous
11. Said or thought by some people to be the stated bad or illegal thing, although you have no proof
12. Fashionable and interesting
13. Able to be obtained, used, or reached
14. Ability to do an activity or job well
15. Limited to only one person

Across

1. Harmed or spoiled
2. Shaped like a ball or circle
3. Boring
4. Complicated and difficult to solve
5. Unusual and unexpected
6. Not bitter or salty
7. Attractive or pleasant
8. Not the same

Down

9. Hard or firm
10. Not guilty of aparticular crime
11. Feeling extreme dislike
12. Behave like adults
13. Grand very large
14. Man
15. No water or other liquid in
16. Extremely surprising, very good, extremely surprised
17. Officer
18. Drinking too much alcohol

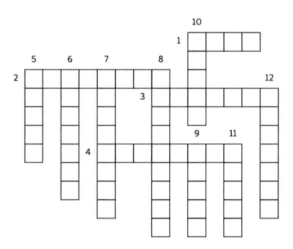

Across

1. Not in danger or likely to be harmed
2. Avoids risks
3. Attractive in appearance
4. Happy and positive

Down

5. Causing pain intentionally
6. Not armed
7. Not guilty of aparticular crime
8. Not wanting others to know
9. Coming before all others
10. Not bitter or salty
11. Telling not the true
12. Revealing

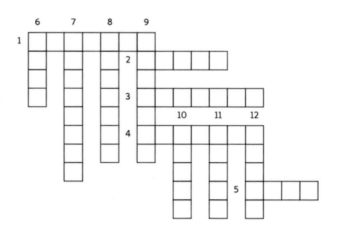

Across

1. Extremely surprising, very good, extremely surprised
2. Develop
3. Attractive in appearance
4. Said or thought by some people to be the stated bad or illegal thing, although you have no proof
5. Not far away in distance

Down

6. Dissolves materials
7. Abnormal, deviant, different
8. A foolish idea
9. Officer
10. Telling not the true
11. Respecting God
12. Drinking too much alcohol

Printed in Great Britain
by Amazon